For my sister Maxine, with love

THE
Newborn
Child

Illustrations first published in *Little One, We Knew You'd Come* by Sally Lloyd Jones,
in the USA by Little Brown and Company and in Great Britain by
Frances Lincoln Children's Books, in 2006
This new edition first published in Great Britain and in the USA in 2016 by
Otter-Barry Books, Little Orchard, Burley Gate, Herefordshire, HR1 3QS

A catalogue record for this book is available from the British Library.

ISBN 978-1-91095-945-9

Printed in China
9 8 7 6 5 4 3 2 1

FSC
www.fsc.org
MIX
Paper from
responsible sources
FSC® C104723

THE Newborn Child

Jackie Morris

Otter-Barry BOOKS

The day the angel came
her life changed forever.

He carried a flower.
He carried a message.

When it was almost time for her child
to be born a call went out across
the land. They travelled far.
A long journey through the desert,
riding in the cool of night,
to pay the taxes all must pay.

As she rode she dreamed
of what he would be like,
her child.

Sleep eluded her. She could feel the child
inside her turn and move. So heavy.
And all the time she wondered
what it would be like to hold him.
Owls kept watch, and the stars,
and the gentle man.

She felt as if she had waited
her whole life for this moment.
Soon.
She knew it would be soon.

He was born while the full moon travelled
across the heavens and the waiting world turned.
She held him close, his skin warm against hers,
in the circle of her mother's love, safe.

Dark hair crowned his head.
Small, perfect hands clenched tight.
Safe in her arms the fragile child rested.
Mine, she thought. A love she had
not known before flowed through her body,
filled her soul.
Mine.

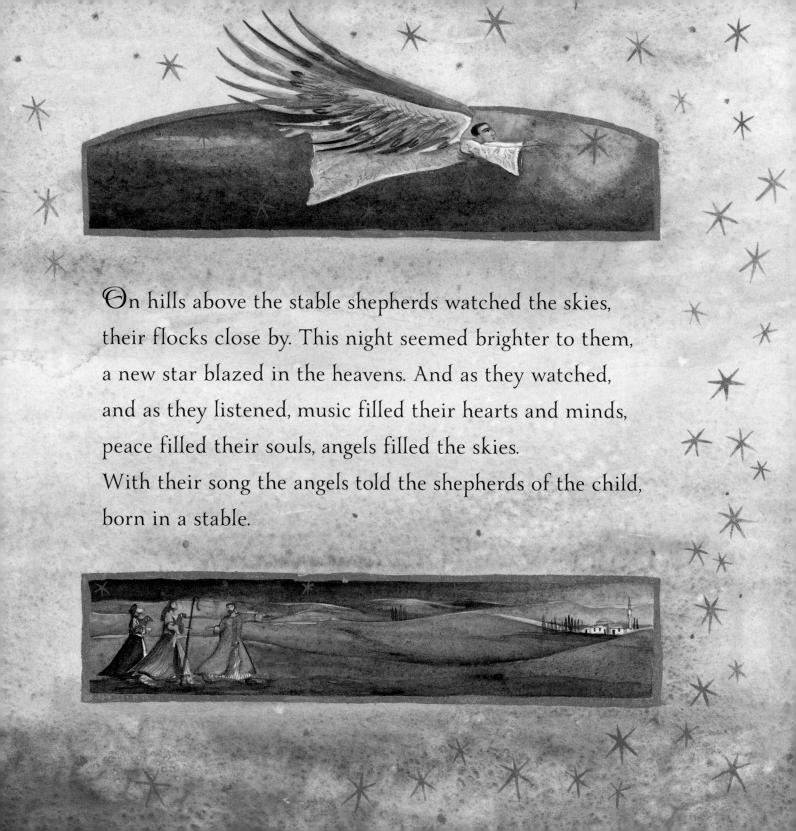

On hills above the stable shepherds watched the skies,
their flocks close by. This night seemed brighter to them,
a new star blazed in the heavens. And as they watched,
and as they listened, music filled their hearts and minds,
peace filled their souls, angels filled the skies.
With their song the angels told the shepherds of the child,
born in a stable.

The shepherds left their flock,
came to find the child, held him
in their great hands, filled with
wonder at this little lamb,
the world's child,
innocent, beautiful.

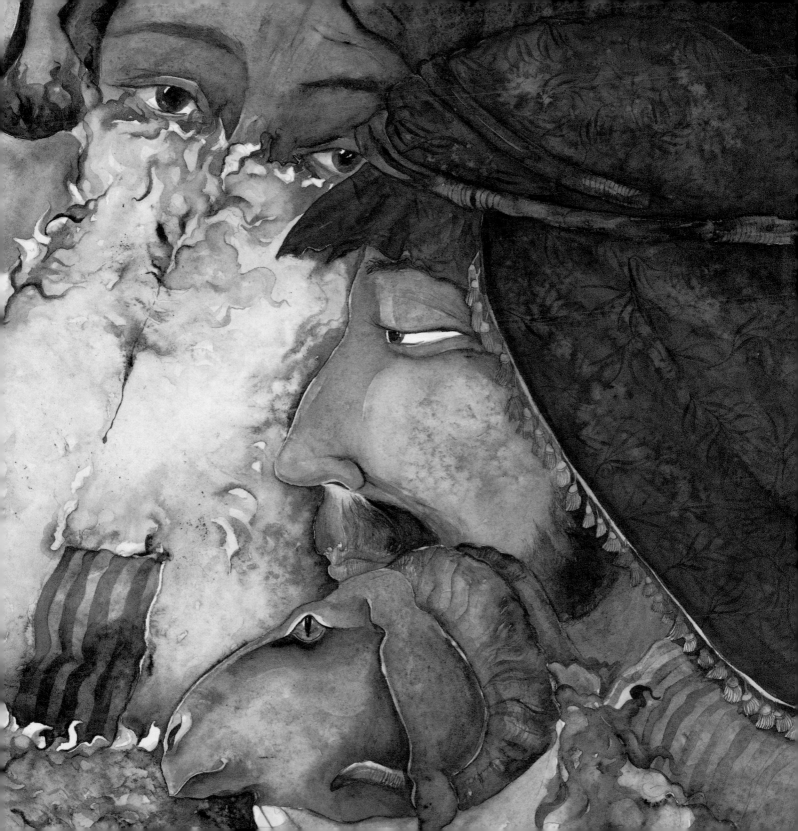

Later, while Mary rested, angels held
the child of love, rocked him gently
in their arms, sang to him a lullaby.

As he slept it seemed the world
was waiting. Butterflies and moths
brushed the air with dusty wings.

From far away three kings travelled, bringing
gifts of gold, frankincense and myrrh.
They had read of the birth of a king in the stars.
They came expecting wealth, a palace.

They found him in a stable. They found him
in his mother's arms. They found real wealth,
true treasure. Love.

They wondered how so much would come
from one so small, so fragile.

How such a one would change the world.

When they were gone Mary once more
held her child close.
A peace descended on the place.
A few small hours were all they had,
alone with the glory of the
newborn child, before the world
came in to claim him.

For now he was just her baby.

For now there was only peace.

For now there was only love.